this american autopsy

CHICANA & CHICANO VISIONS OF THE AMÉRICAS

this
american
autopsy

poems

JOSÉ ANTONIO RODRÍGUEZ

UNIVERSITY OF OKLAHOMA PRESS: NORMAN

This book is published with the generous assistance
of The McCasland Foundation, Duncan, Oklahoma.

Also by José Antonio Rodríguez:
The Shallow End of Sleep: Poems (2011)
Backlit Hour (2013)
House Built on Ashes: A Memoir (2017)

LIBRARY OF CONGRESS CATALOGING-IN-PUBLICATION DATA
Names: Rodríguez, José Antonio, 1974– author.
Title: This American autopsy : poems / José Antonio Rodríguez.
Description: Norman : University of Oklahoma Press, [2019] | Series:
    Chicana & Chicano visions of the Américas series ; volume 23
Identifiers: LCCN 2018057934 | ISBN 978-0-8061-6396-3
    (paperback : alk. paper)
Classification: LCC PS3618.O35835 A6 2019 | DDC 811/.6—dc23
LC record available at https://lccn.loc.gov/2018057934

This American Autopsy: Poems is Volume 23 in the Chicana & Chicano
Visions of the Américas series.

The paper in this book meets the guidelines for permanence and
durability of the Committee on Production Guidelines for Book
Longevity of the Council on Library Resources, Inc. ∞

CONTENTS

acknowledgments / xi

part two. **etiology**

appendix

ACKNOWLEDGMENTS

Grateful acknowledgment is made to the editors and staff
members of the following publications, in which some of the
poems first appeared, sometimes in earlier form:

Connotation Press: An Online Artifact: "Double Glass Doors," "What
we can all do to save my third-world country," "Drug Runner,
or Random South Texas Town"
IthacaLit (online): "Before Stories, or First Memory," "McAllen,
Texas," "Drug Mule"
Luna Luna Magazine (blog): "Liebre en el ejido"
McSweeney's Quarterly Concern: "At the Edge of Omaha"
Memorious (online): "Owl"
The Nation: "Translating an Autopsy, or To the Man Autopsied
into 99 Pages"
The New Yorker: "La Migra"
The Paterson Literary Review: "El Cine Rey: La Ilegal,"
"Challenger," "Hammers and Bricks"
RHINO: "Plutonian Nights," "Poem in honor of the one-year
anniversary of my sister Aleida's death, which is five days away"
Rio Grande Review (online): "Cuando me besan"
The Texas Observer: "American Abundance, or First Trip to H-E-B
Grocery Store"
Upstreet: "Covet," "Knock"

The following anthologies also featured some poems:
(AFTER)life: Poems and Stories of the Dead (edited by Renée M.
Schell, Barbara Froman, and Marta Svea Wallien, Purple
Passion Press, 2015): "Albright-Knox Museum Gift Shop" and
a reprint of "Poem in honor of the one-year anniversary of my
sister Aleida's death, which is five days away"
The Southern Poetry Anthology, vol. 8: *Texas* (edited by William
Wright, Texas Review Press, 2018): "Reynosa"

xi

For insight and community, many thanks to Jean Braithwaite, Sandra Cisneros, Kristi Murray Costello, Liam Costello, Heather Dorn, Augusto Luiz Facchini, Maria Gillan, Carmen Giménez Smith, Leslie Heywood, Sarah Jefferis, Geun-Sung Lee, Melinda Mejia, Jeremiah Crotser, Sarah Pape, Emmy Pérez, Britt Haraway, Riccardo Pizzinato, Friederike Brühöfener, Luis J. Rodríguez, Naomi Shihab Nye, Kim Vose, Joe Weil, CantoMundo, and the Macondo Writers Workshop.

To the editors and staff members at the University of Oklahoma Press, in particular to Kathleen Kelly, thank you for your efforts in support of this work.

A mi madre, mi padre y mis hermanxs, siempre gracias. Al pueblo de la frontera, por su gran humanidad y dignidad, le estaré eternamente agradecido.

"Fear Is a Hurricane," "Holes in Skulls," "From This Parade Float," "This Fourth of July," and "Plutonian Nights" borrow terms from *Words for Empty and Words for Full* by Bob Hicok. "Terrible Things" borrows terms from *Come On All You Ghosts* by Matthew Zapruder. "Ferguson, MO" borrows terms from *Teeth* by Aracelis Girmay.

part one

morphology

A rattlesnake waits
In the grass outside, beside the pig pen.
The snake always hidden, unseen. A field its witness,
The image of a small house away. The corn stalks sing tall
When they music. Hands and feet sink into dirt,
Into cool, into give. The corn all sweetness and milk.
Lying in dirt is like floating in water.
Don't move, and it moves against you.
Movement and stillness
The same act. This is how life breathes
Between the corn stalks. In the dirt
The sky no longer stills as sky, only as blue
Astride the leaves not leaves anymore.
The sun drumming into haze. The real
That belongs to no one. The snake now a curve
Through green.
      Then a voice calls—
            A name begins the world.

Only many houses
Stood flush like train cars
And fences of wire braided
The air to keep out
Stray dogs or stray persons
A stray danger nobody wanted in,
Nobody wanted stopping by, lingering
Visitors had to announce themselves
That side of the fence—an outside—or at least call out
Before lifting the latch
To the gate that girded
The owner's last name spelled
In metal letters: Cortez.

LA MIGRA

The grownups sat on their long chair called couch
And talked of the weather, the dew of the blossoms' morning,
And what might happen to us, the children.
Mom said don't leave the house, not without
Papers. Do I dare speak of the papers hoarded
In corners? How many more poems can you write
About a face spackled with fear before
It holds you? The reader aiming, too.
Let us find a darkened corner, you and I,
Where we will lay these words. Leave children
To sleep in windowless rooms. The mother
Biting a prayer. The country weaving a tomb.

LUCKY

Put him in the last bed at the end of the hallway,
They say in their scrubs, their mouths animated.
They lift the sheet under my body, moving it
To the bed with rails glimmering chrome.

On the other side of the border women who speak
Something other than Spanish walk with babies strapped
To their backs. The babies look sleepy and I think of sun,
The curve of their bodies soft inside fabric.
Everything touching the source, the womb still pulsing
Through the mother's back.

Distorted reflections of limbs on rails entrance my hands—
A cartoon, a clown mirror at a carnival.
Somebody in a white coat says, I am going to push this
Up your nose and down your throat,
To pump your stomach. Can you understand me?
Then spasms, drool wetting my shirt, my chest.
When I wake, only the hissing of the machines colors
The space around me. I throw up a puddle of black tar,
And lie still beside it.

POEM IN HONOR OF THE ONE-YEAR ANNIVERSARY OF MY SISTER ALEIDA'S DEATH, WHICH IS FIVE DAYS AWAY

And which is not really a poem.
But if I call it one, may I be allowed
A small measure of madness? May I
Speak of the urn then with its delicate
Etchings of leaves—silvered vessel that holds
A fragment of what's left. So small,
It fits in my palm.
Wanted each to have a part of her.
May I speak of this detail:
The one-pound bag of shelled pecans—
So many halved hearts—she brought
My parents every time she visited,
Because they savored them so,
Because she knew they'd never spend
On such an extravagance? May I speak
Of the light in that room?
Her hands five days before?
The thinnest fingers. A stillness.
May I speak of the syringe?
Or would that be too much. Morbid.
I know, I know, people die. Except,
Sometimes we don't, like the day before
She died, when my car was totaled
On some nameless street, the other driver
Off to the hospital, the wreckage
Strapped to the bed of a tow truck,
And me walking away.

I leaned on the fence and pretended
    To look at the sun that was burning past the roof
        Of the house the neighbors were tearing down,
Busy with hammers the size of bats,
    Beating it bruised, breaking it brick by brick
        Like ants frenzied on green before a hard rain.
They had started at the bottom
    Without ladders, before the highest bricks
        Moved, came alive, falling on them
Becoming the wall that crumbles
    Erasing the doorway and half burying a son
        And his mom. She, limbs whittled down
To a housedress thin with age,
    Head-bleeds. Somebody yells
        Alcohol! Alcohol!
And soon she is pouring the bottle's contents
    On her head, like a second baptism. A thin red
        Runs down her face. She does not scream.
Too old, too tired.
    The boy, ashen then, dragged to the hospital
        Ends up on crutches.
The grownups sit on the front porch
    Talk about the woman's strange behavior
        The broken boy's slow recovery. Why the large hammers?
Another son works in Chicago, has a good job,
    Will build them a new house. Lucky them,
        The grownups say.
Brick houses never tilt but fall
    And their fall is angry because they cannot bend
        Into the ground slow like a minute hand.
That's what I thought sometimes, then, though I knew
    Houses don't get angry.
        They just get old.

FAGGOT

I recognized the word
When I heard it
In the school yard
With the monkey bars
And the fields that burned brown
Where the coach
Teamed us to play dodgeball.
The roughest boys, with the hair cut askew,
With the name-calling,
Played the best.
Always windy and the voices
Staggered. When I answered
To the name, when I turned
To the sound of the word,
They cut letters into trees.

Someone knocked at the door and we all turned our heads.
    The Challenger exploded, the principal said.
    The astronauts are dead. Turn on your TV.
The newscaster solemn with his perfect hair.
You cannot see the astronauts in the image.
You cannot hear them. They are tiny inside
That huge ship that itself looks tiny inside the TV screen.
I think this is supposed to be sad,
But I can't picture the astronauts dying,
Can't even picture their tiny screams. They were excited,
Then they weren't.
Like every night, when I lie in bed
Mumbling the chores for the following day,
Until I don't, though I don't know when.
The news keeps airing the video, like a drill.
And like a drill, we learn it.
The shuttle then resembling a toy, a flying saucer
Rising into the blue, until it transformed into a cloud of white,
Foamy streams like firecracker snakes that reached the edge
And were gone.

In the film a woman huddles
Cramped in a hollow inside
Baled hay in the bed of a pickup.
The coyote runs
Into border patrol agents
And she knows to be
Perfectly quiet.
The baby in her arms
Begins to cry.
To keep them
From getting caught,
She covers the baby's face
With her hand.
The agents hear nothing,
Wave all of this through,
She knows because
The truck begins moving
Again, though the baby won't.
She has smothered
The life from the fragile body.
An accident.
The other woman
In the hollow,
The film's star,
In almost complete darkness,
Stares with luminous eyes
At the lifeless
Then looks away.

First the local news: young man down
For spring break, gone missing, his body
Found days later mutilated in Matamoros,
White boys' party town across the border.
A new limb every day, a sacrifice of flesh
To gods in exchange for invulnerability—
Cartels witching immunity from bullets even,
With a cauldron and its sediment.
Mark was the first American victim:
A photo flashed across our afternoons,
On every channel so young like silk so blond,
Matamoros held up on TV screens, national news,
Map of south Texas, map of Mexico
Floating on the shoulders of men
With history textbook surnames and baritone vowels,
Men palling with presidents.
Men naming the towns we knew,
The places we'd driven through,
Bridges we'd crossed into another country.

Fear is a hurricane
Thrashing the night
That lashes my back
Already bruised
And waiting
For the tinny morning.
Inside this room
Marked with scars,
Symbols fall into drawers.
Feverish. Drum the hours
Until the wreck, I sing
Into my ears
Like a mother might,
While trees nearly dead
Punctuate the rooted world outside.

Holes in skulls,
To search the what of men
That Dahmer dreamt in his bed.
Research getting bestial,
Sometimes getting bit
By bit. Three-sixteenths,
The drill gunning
For this:
    Against which beauty,
    The blade factory tooling
    The unimagined hands?
    And when the sky seems to say yes,
    The moment is not work, but life
    Before the scream bound,
    Then crushed.

AMERICAN DREAM, OR VISITING
MY SISTER'S FANCY HOME

The ceiling slants over the mantel
Of a fireplace never used, fire set pristine.
The large windows look out to the backyard
Where the pool's reflections undulate.
Her sofas shimmer a delicate white,
Which means you can't really sit on them.
She leads us to the family room with an old couch
And open space from which you can see
The breakfast table and chairs made of iron.
    She's got a cool government office job
Like her handsome husband.
    The day before we leave
They say they are trying to get pregnant.
He does most of the talking. Mom says it's
About time to end the selfishness. She smiles
Like she has to. Yeah, we think it's about time,
She murmurs. Then she gets up to fidget in the kitchen.

    The day we leave
I take one last look at the living room,
Pristine as the memory of wedding flowers.
Everything untouched, like a relic or a promise.
Their bedroom. The bed gargantuan,
Kingtall and plush, the frame gray metal,
Mean against the mattress soft,
Bed posts that rise from all corners
And form a canopy of sharp angles, like a cage.
When we leave, I hug her hard.
She says thank you for coming.
I say take care, thank you for everything.

FROM THIS PARADE FLOAT

Pour this bucket of flags fit for
Faces in a carnival crowd—like stillborn life,
Like hope gone out.

Backdoor wasp days.
Chewed-off chambers
Of the nest born from wood. Kneeling
Chambers, larvae parasitic.
Voice of the hinge their anthem.
Phantom memory collective,
A country dreamed into monolith.

Democracy is the smell
Of hotdogs, the haunted smiles.
Mind the hands and worship the feverish
Home. Write politic freedom into an x,
Claim nature by a holy star.

Ideas are only consensus.
A field beyond the backdoor,
Tongs in one hand, a beer in the other.
Taste that which feels whole—
The snap of firewood, the flesh,
The untethered fire.
Speech burning the air,
Frenzy of wasps.

THE FIRED GUN

The theater's basement intimate, a quiet
Like the visitor that won't leave,
Tastefully hued museum-smooth walls,
Installations busy with track lights
For the fossilized documents with scribbles,
Frail and dated newspaper clippings,
Map of the town around the theater, the dotted line
Tracing the actor's escape, the fired gun
A perfect product of metal molds,
And the pillow bloodstained
To traces of rust.
    Death is the patriot's carnival
    And here the star attraction:
    Behind glass the murmur
    Of Lincoln's last breath.

FOR TAMIR RICE, WHOM I NEVER MET

Think shower of morning
Drone through closed curtains,
Language of toothbrush and toothpaste.
A small sink, space for cupped hands.
Green space and the imagined bullet.
Think arms above your head. Arms above.
Trivial sound meaning knot,
Meaning surrender the vital
Of you. Then the head there,
Altar to the body thrum-less.
In the news, a nation people him.
In the news, the autopsy of spring.

TERRIBLE THINGS
—after Matthew Zapruder

Moving thought dreams
Actually breeze
Across the city.
Periodically someone's body
Births feelings
That conjure something like
A room in a house,
And its story—
    Memory's account—
Sits on the couch
While vital wants
Do terrible things
To the walls,
Like believe.

PLUTONIAN NIGHTS
—after Bob Hicok

Plutonian nights
Light a thousand margaritas.
A thousand fools exchange
The yes, begin to glass the rain.
Gunfire-close, they raze
A rainforest saying
Something impossible.
Bulbs spring, blushing the sky.
They'd like to touch
The river's decibels, something
Like sipping the life of a poem.

Night chills the world into silence and the city churns. I'm
carrying the day's chores in the front door when I see you
scrounging through my garbage, hear you say looking for
paints. I wonder how it came to be that you stand there. Come
sit on the porch, I say, and you oblige. You know, *Sunflowers* now
hangs in London's National Art Gallery and your self-portrait
hangs in New York City's Met, I offer. That's not why I did it,
you say. Sounding like my late grandfather. I read about you in
grade school, I say, saw *Starry Night* in the textbook, and even
muted on the page, all of it dwarfed on my lap, I knew then
the dance of beauty and despair, the way one can redeem the
other. You turn to me, your hands on your knees, and stare.
I tell you about the Albright-Knox museum in Buffalo, how it
doesn't hang any of your paintings, but in the gift shop's kid
section dolls of famous painters nest in wicker baskets: Dali in
cape, Kahlo in braids, Picasso in sailor stripes, and Van Gogh,
twelve inches of stuffed felt, with a detachable ear. Velcroed. So
children may play with the cut and cleave of you. Look at the
light, you say, see it descend on the asphalt, how it scintillates,
how it wants to love you.

STILL LIFE WITH *VIEW FROM THE WINDOW*
AT LE GRAS AND *GONE WITH THE WIND* HAIR-COLOR
TEST AT HARRY RANSOM CENTER

Is this what becomes of the object that signaled the future?
An image more grim than grainy of shadows as stand-ins

For the human form and a wall that speaks geometry.
The display drowning in a dark cured a little by a blacklight—

The first image trapping light on metal is now protected from it—
Threatened by that which it once caught and wrestled into contour.

The more photographs we take, the less the mind retains
In the house of memory. And the graph illustrating the proliferation

Of photo-taking points to a future where we may forget our own faces
With too many mirrored reminders. Beyond the dead-blue booth

Is the next installation: footage of Clark Gable and Vivien Leigh
In costume standing together, eyes to camera. Filmmakers seeking a match

For their hair colors, finding the most compatible shades,
The ones closest to their reality. Having seen the movie,

I recognize them instantly, though what's most peculiar
Is their gaze. Scarlett and Rhett photographed at twenty-four

Frames per second. Every image fretted over. Half smiles on a loop.
Their hands for a second on each other's cheeks, mimicking affection.

AMERICAN ABUNDANCE, OR FIRST TRIP
TO H-E-B GROCERY STORE

Carnation milk can sat
On the shelf in the store:
The reddest flower copying itself
Over and over—so many perfect bouquets
At the same edge and no counter
Between them and me.

I feared they might go bad, spoil,
Because surely nobody could,
No matter how hungry, empty this landscape
Where magic repeated itself over every tile.

Having been allowed to hold
Every bag and box, every sum, in my hands
And place them in a wheeled cart,
Without anyone to say no,
To demand payment, I asked Mom
If we could just walk out,

Take it all home. But no,
There was the young woman in uniform.
And her steady hands passed every item
Over a clear window by the register
With a red eye that beeped.
And on the other side,

Every item dropped tilted and rolled,
Revealing the mark—a block of lines like prison bars
And numbers with hard corners—
The code by which to pass the scanner
Like a bridge.

COVET

During recess—boys and girls antsy
By the monkey bars—he took out his wallet,
Paid me the dollar. In class, seated in front of me,

He propped his elbows on his desk, leaned forward
As if reading the math worksheet I'd answered for him.
The light a cape draping his broad shoulders.

His back to me, I guessed him wondrous
At my marks on that white sheet of paper—
The language only I knew. His lips slightly parted,

Buck teeth out and loud. On walls bordering
Our discrete islands hung the poster board
With our names and varying quantities of gold stars,

The alphabet with an animal for every letter,
And the flag stoic as a statue. All demanding love.
To covet them was supposed to be enough,

But it never was—everything out there far
From our little desks facing forward
Where we tried to discern
What the world would covet in us.

CUANDO ME BESAN

El frío que se ha paseado
Por el solar baldío
Al lado de mi casa de ochenta años
Cubierta de gusanos que susurran
Todas las noches escuetas
Sin quinceañeras ni cuetes

Se cola por entre los olanes
De las cortinas floreadas
Sin orugas ni mariposas.

Abrazo las sábanas mojadas entre
El parpadeo de mis sueños
Que hierben con lagartijos
Como las playas de las islas Galápagos
Y el algodón
    O el recuerdo de lo que fue
    Flaco como el niño tisiquiento del otro lado
Se deja
Y toma de mis babas el calor
De la saliva para ofrecérmelo después
Mohoso pero tibio,
    Untándolo en mi piel de lunares como meteoritos

Porque sus fibras cansadas
Y moldeadas por cuerpos como hojas del elote
Saben de mi padre y su espalda
Mi padre y sus callos
Mi padre y sus manos
      Como costales viejos
Que me estrujan
Cuando me besan
Cuando me estrujan.

part two

etiology

LIEBRE EN EL EJIDO

Por fin sale de su pozo
Y su cuerpo acurrucado
Se tizna con el humo desganado
De la basura que mis padres queman
Por la húmeda tarde,
Ante la vista de los vecinos.

Olfatea el plástico del envase
Que se retuerse entre las llamas
Como chicharrones de cerdo
Y cierra los ojos. Empieza
A caminar como una anciana.
No sé de sus años en el pozo.

Las parcelas se achican
Ante las anchas carreteras.
La acequia se hace chorro
Y el panteón se cree rey
Con tantas coronas.
Ni siquiera voltea a ver

Los trozos de papa
Que tengo en mi mano.
Se va porque no quiere probar
Las escarchas rosadas de mi casa.
¿Debo también celebrar su partida?

Aquí no se celebran los cumpleaños
Porque llaman al recuerdo del nacimiento
Prueba de la concepción
    Que jamás se piensa—
Como el sabor del terrón desmoronado
Entre los dientes. Las velas se encienden
Sólo en la iglesia.

La liebre se va
y el panteón se burla de mí.

We sat conscious of hands clasped, and that's how the nurse
put it, soft and tactful with an artificial citrus scent: *Your father
is having a heart attack.* Not: *had a heart attack.* Not: *impending
heart attack.* Though he wouldn't die that day, not in a hospital
bed. No one pictured it: his body flanked by chrome rails.
The double glass doors sealing in the smell of medical
plastics. And how could a father's body disappear like that,
with his hands painting the space in which he breathed?
He'd been mowing someone else's lawn, heaved the mower
onto the pickup truck, drove home, threw up, and someone
said call an ambulance. But I drove instead. Grabbed a towel
should he vomit again. And he didn't whistle on the way that
was all green lights.

WHAT WE CAN ALL DO TO SAVE
MY THIRD-WORLD COUNTRY

Support the donkey show economy
Enjoy a Nestlé jar of cold jarro beans
Taste the watermelon sweat
Sell your camera phones to wetbacks
Sign the curandera's appointment ledger
Rub your palm on this doe-eyed rosary
Swallow little girls' citrus sweet
Pander to half-moon erections
Trade in mercury bracelets
Drink the mesquite sap off babies' fingers
Purge the stomachs of nopales
Suckle from my wet bedsheets
Rent my mother's soot-covered hands
Witness my father's hunched back
Read me your Alamo story
Save me in your CK jeans and velvet cowboy hats
See me gnaw with teeth made of corn
Count the cancer moles on my back
Taste the head of the rattlesnake
Kiss the gray waste of sexed factories
Euthanize the silver mines
Feed me the salty semen of your lucent gods
Play Mexican bingo with the ghosts of abandoned homes

DRUG MULE

How easy, you wouldn't think
And they almost come to life
Right past the teeth. Foolish
I wish they were,
So much depending on my insides,

My will to hold and carry
Until satisfaction—almost,
Shall I say it, like giving birth.
Only a few pounds of magic.

And yet multitudes walk away
From the named world, vessels now
Only open mouths. My body
Will heave their sustenance—
An insipid nourishment.

Now the laying of hands.
That wait. Now my bowels—yes,
Gold is what I've become.

Heard the men in suits
Said no to Target, to Best Buy,
To all those indoors
With cool-heeled bodies
Pelting you with khaki smiles
And the latest trinket. Heard
The men in suits didn't want
Traffic, a lit world.
The rich don't mind
The dark, don't even fear
It when it floats in every magic
Their hands tremble for,
The bad shit I hear makes you
Not even want to fuck.
I've seen the tight heft of it
Glisten, moonlight touching
The tight corners of truck beds.
Drive it there, they say,
And don't ask questions.
And when the cop car twinkles
Its lights from some bank
Sluggish with night,
I know they like to play it like that.
No indoor job for me,
Nothing but the soothing silence,
The road past midnight,
Every body learning to wait.

KNOCK

—According to news accounts, the drug cartels have moved into the isolated rural villages along the Mexican border with the United States.

There's the knock again,
Always a startle
Though I hear it all night,
All the moments of my waking life.

The sizzle of the potatoes,
The resigned simmer of the beans
Wedge between the rustle as they settle,
Dumb at what the next moment might bring
With torturers eating from my table—
Boots, workshirts, and weathered belts guzzling coffee.

I don't tremble anymore or stutter.
Every next minute is a ghost I inhabit.
Dios me perdone
Dios me perdone
Dios me perdone,
But I'm running out of prayers.

Where might my loved one be,
Cariño de mis cariños long past
Some other sliver of water perhaps,
Behind another iron wall,
While my tortillas go to these strangers
With a stare like all of them is bloodshot.

You never know how the love you save
Will spill like heat leaving a griddle
When all is done. When the last of them
Leave to their labors, and I return
To bed, the knock in my ears
Like the cruelest word.

OWL

—*In Nogales, Arizona, a special large refrigerated room
has been built to hold the numerous bodies of the undocumented
who die trying to cross the desert.*

They think I'm uninhabited,
Having settled me
Into this zippered coffin,
But I wait, because soon I know
All will be released
Out of this darkness
So like the desert night—
The saguaros dumb giants
Reaching eager for the sky
With both hands.
The owls perched half inside them
With those eyes like dry wells,
As if all the stars are never enough.
Starving for light.
What did the elders say
They were? Guides?

And the yelp
Of the coyote morphing
Into an infant's cry, filled
With such longing, I wondered
What country I'd stepped into.
Even this machine in the shape
Of a room seems to murmur
Lonesome, so made in the image of man,
It too breathes sorrow.
But I am already leaving.
Can hardly hear it anymore.

I'm nervous, I say
Over dinner
In a Holiday Inn.
Nothing to be
Nervous about, says
My colleague who's already testified.
Tomorrow you say
Yes, I'm the one
Who translated
Those phone calls.
And she rolls
Her eyes, relishes
Another morsel
Of Salisbury steak and potatoes.

Here I wish
More than anything
That I could be
Her, convinced that this
Entire enterprise
Crowned by a judge
And his gavel
Is a mere formality,
That the men in orange
Are crash-test dummies,
That the defense attorneys
Are performers
Playing at picking apart
The terms I chose
For the entertainment
Of the courtroom audience.

But what if
I mess it up, I say.
What if I say
The wrong thing,
Lose the case.
Some expert I'd be,
Then.
    Won't matter,
    She says,
    They're Mexican
    And on trial
    In the Bible Belt.
    They don't stand a chance.

Is a black and white photograph of Bonnie. That Bonnie.
And Clyde. Sulking inside the picture frame. Between them,
the story clustered in clipped phrases: Lawmen capture bank
robbers. Bonnie could be Faye Dunaway and Clyde, Warren
Beatty. They slouch over the Ford and wink days before the
rain, days before the bullets, the way film seduces the eye—
quick cuts, flashes of bodies whole until the climax shrapnel
sharp. In the lounge Bonnie and Clyde pose as if for this
collage, homage to the men who lurk behind the hedge.
Down by the edge, a list of banks. In the film, Clyde already
criminal rescues a baby-blonde Bonnie from her dead-end
afternoons behind a porch screen, later crowning her with
a chic beret. In the lounge the Bureau monuments the end
of their spree under a gush of gunfire. Against the wall of
the lounge a frame: Bonnie and Clyde and the triggers. The
brittle real in film bleached by the camera flash, a half smile
over her lips only. Another photo the site of the ambush,
in the lounge with the office fridge and its Post-Its. Clyde
killed his first person in prison, an inmate who raped him.
Remember to grip the gun, Bonnie liked to write inside the
hem of her skirt.

REYNOSA

And now the wailing
City, how it howls
Accordions
Onto alleys, sings
Cans of warm beer,
Dishes brown breast
And tongue.
Foster mother
To all boys on buses
From dirt
Towns mourning
Their dying farms.

Sometimes at night
I hear the bridge
Buckle with the petulant
Weight of labor,
Hear the gun chafe
Against thigh uniformed
In polyester. Holstered.
And the knowing chuckle.

Then the city
Cynical—a membrane
Permeable, a conduit for magic
Too rich for us
Before the tallest wall.

TO THE SIXTEEN-YEAR-OLD SHOT
BY THE BORDER PATROL AGENT

This is not a poem
Not a poem
Not a poem this
Is a call to say
The bridge should have fallen
Long ago, the bridge
Should have never been
Barb wired
Never been
Manned with dogs
A call to say I remember
To say I cannot not remember
The rush of the river
That chants your name
In a foreigned tongue
A call to say that in the vision
I stand by you
Stone in hand
And the arc of the hurl
The stone's trajectory
Is its own banner

This is not a poem not for you
Not when home is what you surrendered
Boy of no country
I have burned the papers
That call you human trafficker
I have memorized
The name of the uniformed
I have found where he claims home
And every morning
Before work I walk by
And leave a rock
At his front door.

SELF-PORTRAIT WITH DISCO BALL AND DUST DEVIL
—after Eduardo Corral

I am blacklight and smirk.
I am nylon
And legend. I am
Gulping the swirl of mossy river
Through my eyes
Like a magic trick.
In my hands
    Crayons
    And quills. I am
Conducting an interview
With my outline
On the bed.
My spine tickles
My skull
A hollow space,
    Potential. I'm dancing

A tornado:
A Russian prodigy. I am
Fractal and hologram
I'm muscle
And delight. I'm dangling
From a bough
Noosed into blue.
Gnats in my eyes. I remember
What the masters
Forgot: A monument is a tree
    Standing after a fire.
I'm satire
Disguised as parable
A gladiator
Before the minister's hand.

I kneel, a grackle perches
On my shoulder.
I snatch it and bite into its wing.
My breath lingers iridescent.
I'm totem pole
And hieroglyph

I'm crimson
And turquoise.
My voice dismantles
A rosary into beads
Of sweat. I am dust devil
And thrash. I'm
Naked as myth.
I'm rhinestone and swagger.
    My laughter
Spins above the crowding of ants
Like a disco ball.

Falsetto and bass.
I'm hurling every note.

I'm full-throated and sublime
Straddling a stallion.

Club lights twirl
    From the tallest mesquite.
I square dance a riddle.

TRANSLATING AN AUTOPSY, OR TO THE MAN
AUTOPSIED INTO 99 PAGES

Please know that I read them all and could not weep, afraid
to compromise the task I was handed: to reconstitute this
you in the Spanish tongue. Know that I aimed to honor what
the body told, to tell the Mexican police of the pages with
the rudimentary outline of a male body the size of an action
figure with wounds marked X on your torso, evidence of
the knife, pages with the coroner's notes a jumble of semi-
legible jargon of anatomy atomized into dorsal and proximal,
posterior and anterior, inches and centimeters of distance and
depth conquered by the killer's thrum and slash, pages with
the crime scene scribbled into a living room couch soaked
through, blood crusting the floor and telling of drought,
splatters on the wall dripping every synonym of pain, pages
with interviews of neighbors who saw the many men who
came and went, the rumor of your inclinations for one, the
one who may have been the one who fled to Mexico, pages
with hands, even your hands, even the cut and pierce of your
hands, telltale signs of the struggle against annihilation, flesh
screaming mercy, your hands and the word *manos* recalling
the word *hermanos*, which is how you may have seen each other
once, before the first kiss.

At the subatomic level, simultaneous presence and absence
is possible.

The early peoples of Australia, joints swollen after journeys
to a particular cavern, warned of a monster that should
never be awakened. They never called it uranium.

A company has signed a one-thousand-year contract to
handle the waste produced by the Chernobyl disaster.

Queen Elizabeth fought apartheid in South Africa by letting
a black woman hug her.

Albert Einstein imagined trains and passengers when
discovering the relativity of time.

Van Gogh did in fact slice his entire ear off, not just a sliver.

Jim Henson was skeptical of Western medicine.

Oliver Stone relied on his baseball skills at least once when
hurling a grenade in Vietnam.

Up until recently, arson experts summoned by courts knew
dangerously little about the behavior of fire.

The Pax Romana was actually not peaceful.

The question of Jesus Christ's actual existence is irrelevant to
scholars of theology.

According to quantum physics, we are mostly matter-less.

BRILLIANCE

A polar bear is shot
After swimming two hundred miles
In search of food.
A giraffe tethered
To the bed of a truck
Crushes her head on an overpass.
A family of elephants
Drinks from a poisoned pond,
And is heard no more.
The poachers human like you,
Reader, like me with this language
We've invented,
This territory. Primate. Mammalian.

A human child visits a zoo
To discover wonder and, later,
The price of life familiar and foreign,
Because of these words, they'll be told—
Unique and brilliant.

When Dad left to look for work,
The orchards he had tended—
Now burnt by the ice of a December cloud—
Didn't miss him,
And the orange that he otherwise would have stolen
And chilled in the fridge
To later segment for all of us
Like edible love
Remained on the imaginary tree that survived.

The linoleum cracked under his flea market suitcase.
I imagined the mice then still under the floor
And I didn't cry, not because I wouldn't
But because I didn't know to.
Even such displays must be modeled.

All this I have imagined
Because I don't actually remember when he left,
Only that one day he did not sit at the table
And the hollow filled my hands
With a sorrow quiet like the anonymous tree
Leaning on the window
Frail in the winter wind, and fruitless.

FERGUSON, MO
    —after Aracelis Girmay

Jacaranda purple streets. Ceaseless dawn.
Hearts falling like oil blooms.
Admit this blood gone, these flowers burned.
Demigods animating the remnants of petals.

FIRST HAIKU

Know of fathers, Face-
Book? The one I called mine has
Died. What a sentence.

ANTARCTICA

I'm waiting for the screens'
Talking heads, cheeks red and engorged,
To stop bobbing, to quiet
Until only mute faces linger
            Unblinking and quenched.
I'm waiting I think
For the world to empty of words
Like one of those lakes in Antarctica
That develops a crevice in its belly
And dissolves in hours,
A lake older than mountains
Rushing to the great center—
        That imagined place—
Leaving behind the form of its absence.

UNNAMED IN McALLEN, TEXAS

And the children
And the cages
And the children
To the cages
And the man in green
And the cages
And the children play
In the cages
Because they are five
In the cages
And the man in green
Takes a stroll after lunch
By the cages
The lights on all night
In the cages
The lights fall
Over silvery sheets
In the warehouse

Three days they say
To the cages
Only three days
Until the tent city
In the desert
And the hands cling
And the fingers curl
Around the chain link
Of the cages
The hands waiting to touch
In the cages
Waiting to love
Past the cages the fathers and mothers
The hands gripping a paper
With a mother's image
A photocopy
In the cages
Not allowed to love
In the cages

appendix

WHEN THEY KISS ME
— *English translation of "Cuando me besan"*

The cold that has wandered
Through the empty field
By my eighty-year-old house
Covered in worms that murmur
Every night barren
Of quinceañeras and fireworks

Sifts through the curtains'
Floral folds absent of
Caterpillars and butterflies.

I hug the wet bedsheets
In the blink of my dreams
That simmer with lizards
Like the shores of the Galapagos Islands,
And the cotton
    Or the memory of what it was,
    Skinny like the sickly kid on the other side,
Lets me
And takes from my drool
The heat of my saliva to offer it back
Now musty but warm,
    Spreading it on my skin with moles like meteorites,

Because its fibers tired
And molded by bodies like husks
Know of my father and his back
My father and his calluses
My father and his hands
    Like worn-out burlap
That grip me
When they kiss me
When they grip me.

HARE OF THE EJIDO

— *English translation of "Liebre en el ejido"*

Finally rises from its burrow
And its crouching body
Is colored in soot by the aimless smoke
Of the trash my parents burn
In the humid evening,
Before the neighbors' eyes.

It sniffs the plastic of the bottle
That warps amid the flames
Like pork rinds
And closes its eyes. It moves
Like an old woman.
I know nothing of its years in the burrow.

The portioned fields diminish
Before the widening highways.
The waterway becomes a trickle
And the cemetery thinks itself king
With so many crowns.
Won't even turn to see

The chunks of potato
In my hand.
It turns, refusing to taste
The frost over my pink house.
Must I also celebrate its leaving?

Here we do not celebrate the birthdays
That recall the memory of the birth,
Proof of conception
    That is never acknowledged—
Like the taste of dirt, clod crumbling
Between my teeth. The candles are lit
Only at church.

The hare hobbles away
And the cemetery laughs at me.